I0150656

MARY TELLS THE
NATIVITY STORY
of Prophecies Fulfilled

A Book of Joy for All Seasons

VANESSA WEBBE

Extra MILE Innovators
Kingston, Jamaica W.I

. . . . .

Published by
Extra MILE Innovators
54 Montgomery Avenue
Kingston 10, Jamaica W. I.
www.extramileja.com

Cover Design: Ravishankararya and Pro-designer Olivia
Illustrator: Ravishankararya

DISCLAIMER: This book is written using the accounts of the story of the birth of Jesus recorded in Luke chapters one and two and Matthew one and two as well as prophecies concerning his birth from the book of Genesis, Isaiah and Micah. Other books in the Bible used for reference were Job, Psalms, Haggai, and Malachi. Scripture references are taken from the New King James Version of the Bible.

Author Contact:

For feedback and speaking engagements, contact the author at
webbev3@gmail.com

To mom, Bernadine Webbe

Foreword

I am always fascinated at the way mothers tell stories about their children. Neither the occasion nor content change the nuance of a mother's narration. Mothers in their storytelling, are convincing; they are passionate, and their subjectivity is insightful. For the perceptive eye and one who has a penchant for details, the subjectivity of a mother's account is not inadmissible nor unusefully biased, it is a picture into who the mother's offspring really is, beyond a single activity or achievement. Seldom do mothers speak only of a single event, there is an intricately detailed account of the life of that child from conception to event or achievement.

Without dishonouring the biblical narrative structure, Webbe has carefully captured Mary's story in the way a mother would tell it, and presents it to us in a way that not only causes us to see Jesus through Mary's eyes, but also to love him, revere him and wonder at him in the same way Mary does. For nowadays readers traversing a centuries old text, there is a reverent 21st century contextualizing while, at the same time, maintaining the story in both its original context and original written context. Creative. Emotive. Biblical.

—Ricardo O. Henry
Ordained Bishop, Church of God
Tampa, Florida

Introduction

This book explores the Nativity story from Mary's perspective as the mother of Jesus. *In Mary Tells the Nativity Story; of Prophecies Fulfilled*, the voice of Mary is heard sharing her journey through the Nativity as she takes on the role of an apologist. As a mother, she is inspired to share her side of the Nativity story, in response to the unbelief of her people in not accepting Christ as Redeemer and instead calling for him to be crucified. Mary's main aim in sharing the story is to proclaim Jesus as Israel's promised Messiah to the world.

The first draft of this book was written in September of 2017, under lock down on campus "West Hall" dorm, at the University of the Virgin Islands, during the passage of hurricane

Maria. I seized the break from regular class work at the school of business, to release a book that was brewing on the inside.

Delving into the story of the Nativity of Christ, took my mind away for a while, from the horrifying threats of the storm that was passing and even reduced the traumatic stress hurricane Irma caused a few weeks back. The book came to me as a gift to bring unfathomable calm and solitude, during a very challenging period.

I felt the presence of the 'Prince of Peace" in the dormitory, while working on the book. My prayer is that persons reading this book will experience the peace and power of God at work in their lives. As we read about angels appearing with good news, the virgin birth miracle, the escape from Herod's wrath, may we also trust in God to do something supernatural in our own lives.

This book reminds us of God's power and presence at work in our lives to bring His sovereign will to fruition. Mary was a young virgin girl who allowed God to take complete control of her life. While Mary was highly esteemed in the eyes of the Lord, Mary also, highly valued God's plan and purpose for her life. She did not just carry a sticker that says, "I am blessed and highly favoured, she also waved a flag that said, "I surrender Lord."

Mary trusted in God's plan for her life and humbly gave herself to be used as a vessel of honour unto the Lord. The book reminds us of the benefit of saying yes to God, and how so many lives are impacted positively when we say 'yes' to God's will. One young girl said 'yes' to God and opened the door that brought salvation to the world, in God's divine timing.

We are all challenged to listen attentively to the voice that is asking us to carry out that assignment that God has ordained for us. It is that service to God that will make us fulfill our ultimate purpose for mankind that will bring all glory to God.

Each chapter of this book is a brief narrative of Mary's reflection of her journey with Jesus, placing emphasis on the scenes that surrounds his birth. The book includes Mary's account of the angel Gabriel's enunciation, Mary's invigorating visit with her cousin Elizabeth, Joseph's struggle to believe Mary's story about her pregnancy, the birth of Jesus, and relating episodes thereafter.

The case of Jesus' divinity is strengthened in the story as Mary highlights Bible prophecies about the birth of Jesus that she had witnessed come to pass. At the end of her story, readers are encouraged to be mindful of Bible prophecies. Mary calls attention to the angel's words that Jesus will one day return to earth, which were spoken while He was ascending to His father in heaven. She makes an appeal for us to position ourselves to gain a place in Christ's eternal Kingdom, by serving Him now.

There is much food for thought various groups can glean from the book. The theme of relationship and family is strong. Mary's love for her son is evident. A strong bond can be felt between mother and son. God's love for the family certainly resonates in the book. To preserve the young couple's plans for marriage, Jehovah God intervenes at a time Joseph is planning to put away Mary.

God reveals to Joseph in a dream that Mary became pregnant by the work of the Holy Spirit. This intervention shows how much God desires peace and harmony within families. Readers are therefore reminded to rely on God to help solve family problems.

The book also shows how family togetherness is essential, especially when facing obstacles and challenges as Mary and Joseph worked together, in obedience to God, to preserve Jesus' life which was at threat by King Herod. The family is featured as being extremely important to God in the time of Mary and Joseph, as it was at the creation with Adam and Eve and so it must be today since God remains the same yesterday, today and forever. The need for trust in relationship is also featured as Joseph is challenged with the test of trust to believe Mary's story about her pregnancy. Families are also encouraged to trust in God for guidance and protection, to walk in obedience to

God and overcome every plan or plot of the enemy.

While theological discussions on the role of women in ministry is an ongoing debate, the book shows how equally important men and women are in fulfilling God's Kingdom plans. Mary was needed to carry the seed of the Son of God and Joseph was needed to help Mary care, protect, provide for and nurture the Christ child.

Looking at women in service for God, Mary played a pivotal role in bringing God's redemptive plan for mankind into being, joining other women like Ruth and Esther, who foreshadowed in opening doors for redemption.

Further, Ruth can be seen as a woman who played a vital role in saving the family line (from which Jesus came), Esther, saving a nation and Mary saving the world. What is plain to see is that women have been chosen by God to serve in significant Kingdom affairs throughout the history of the Bible.

Mary Tells the Nativity Story of Prophecies Fulfilled is an addition to resources available on

Messianic Prophecies. It is an ideal book for the family devotion table as well as a gift for someone who is asking questions about Jesus' Divinity. The book reminds us all of the need to be ready for the return of Christ as it is an eminent prophecy soon to be fulfilled. Once again, we are reminded that God's promises will stand the test of time.

Sunday school teachers can use the book to discuss the various scenes of the Nativity story. The book is an inspiring material for women's group to celebrate God's love and calling on their lives, even when others are still debating women's role in society and ministry.

Mary Tells the Nativity Story of Prophecies Fulfilled reminds us that God has a special plan and purpose for each of us. We each have a role to play that will bring benefit to others. It does not matter how insignificant you think your role maybe, it is interconnected, your action can contribute to someone's salvation. God chooses the role that is best for us, hence we can say *yes* to his calling, as He equips the called.

Most times people don't know what they are best at until God calls them into service for Him and they answer the call. The book is urging us to see ourselves as valuable vessels to be used by God. God has placed a seed inside of us for His honour and glory.

Like Mary, we too should cherish the seed that has been planted in our wombs and allow it to spring up, bringing benefit to many. Ideally, we want the seed to grow as the mustard seed Jesus likened to the Kingdom of heaven, therefore becoming a huge, mature tree with many branches providing shade, food and shelter to others (Matthew 13:31-32; Mark 4:30-32; Luke 13:18-19).

This book also points out that God is faithful to fulfill His purpose through us. He will stand at our side and abide with us when we abide with Him. We are reminded, when we are called into service by God, it does not mean a rosy path, but empowerment to go through, to jump over walls and leap over obstacles.

God will protect us, watch over us and bring us through victoriously, though we may have to face the adversary. Through reading the book, believers are encouraged to hold on to God's promises for their lives. Those who have not yet come to faith in Jesus are encouraged to search the Scriptures for the truth about Christ and to prepare for His imminent return.

CONTENTS

1.

Mary's Testimony

"Therefore, the Lord Himself will give you a sign: Behold,
the virgin shall conceive and bear a Son..."
(Isaiah 7:14 NKJV).

"My soul magnifies the Lord" has been my song of praise, since the announcement of the news of His birth. The paradox though, I have to confess, knowing my people rejected, Jesus, as our Redeemer, brought sorrow to my heart. The scene of a malevolent mob before me, berating my son, shouting loudly their ill wish for him to be crucified, was beyond unbearable but God knows how to lift us up when we are in the valley. To comfort my heart, from the horrifying scenes, my heavenly Father, flipped the pages of my mind, miles away back in time.

Precious memories flooded my mind of the most memorable days of my life, the miracles surrounding the birth of our Messiah. How very privileged I was to be chosen to be the mother of the Christ Child, the Son of God. There was never a child more precious than the one I held in my bosom; His name is Jesus, the Christ, the Saviour of the world. He who is King of kings and Lord of lords, I once cradled in my arms. He came humbly, as a tiny bundle of joy and beauty, yet, he came as Immanuel, God with us, in all power, glory and splendour. Of course, I was intrigued with the mystery of the incarnation.

Many people say that they do not believe that my son, Jesus, was the Messiah. The people refused to believe in Jesus although He showed forth His Father's glory in the wondrous miracles He performed in Israel. I wish, I could stand by my Son and testify to Pilot, to the Chief Priest and to all the unbelievers. The religious leaders called many witnesses to testify and false witnesses they were.

Oh, how I wish they had called me, Jesus' mother, to testify about my son, like the time they called on the parents of the man who was born blind, whom Jesus healed (John 9:1-38). These religious leaders wanted to know for sure that the man born blind was their son and how his eyes were opened. His parents were able to confirm that their son was born blind but that they knew not how his eyes were opened (John 9:20-21). Truly, it was not fair that they did not call on me to speak about my son!

Perhaps I was not called because I am a woman, and the voice of a woman is suppressed and silenced in this world, ruled by men. The religious leaders of the time behaved like mechanical men lacking care and compassion for their people. They seem to seek out opportunities to condemn others based on the Law of Moses, that scarcely any Israelite can keep. In fact, when women are caught breaking the Laws which were given to Moses, we do not have a chance to defend ourselves and seldom can we escape the wrath of judgement.

Seemingly, the Lawkeepers have not opened their hearts to the Law of Love Jesus has established: to love God whole heartedly and to love neighbour as self. Accepting His Law of Love, will eradicate hatred and social injustices as we work towards treating everyone equally, regardless of gender, race or other. In His coming to earth, Jesus gave us the key of love, to help solve most of the world's problems, in families, communities and nations. My Son brought freedom for all; freedom for the dying soul through accepting His gift of salvation and freedom for humanity to enjoy a better world, by accepting His love. Now *that* is the abundant life! Today, I can rejoice because my son, Jesus, during his ministry here on earth, treated us, women, with respect. Thanks be to God! Yes, He, though sinless, refused to cast a single stone at us. He lived out the words He preached. As His beloved John would often repeat, "He did not come to condemn the world, but that the world through Him might be saved" (John 3:17).

Our Messiah showed love for people everywhere He went, and instead of condemning us, He came to us at our hour of need. Ask the woman at the well from Samaria who once had many husbands, or ask Mary Magdalene whose soul was tormented by the evil one, until Jesus came and set her free. Oh, yes, Jesus had done many wonderful things to demonstrate His deity and the glory of His Father in heaven.

At every opportunity, Jesus was busy doing good deeds and showing compassion to the human race He came to deliver. He turned water into wine at the wedding in Cana, He healed the sick, raised the dead to life again, fed the multitude and He made us women feel liberated from the harsh social laws that made us feel like second class citizens. That is why today, I feel bold to tell the story about my son, Jesus. Yes, I Mary, the mother of Jesus, as I sit at the foot of the cross on the Hill of Golgotha also known as Calvary, I know that I can no longer be a silent Hebrew woman. I want everyone to know that He who hung on the cross is indeed the Son of God.

Please, listen to my story, the most incredible story of the birth of our Messiah, then search the Torah, search your hearts, have a conversation with the Heavenly Father and I am certain that the truth will be revealed to you, too. The revelation that God came to earth through His Son, Jesus. You can trust the words of a mother to give a precise account about the birth of her child.

2.

The Appearance of the
Angel Gabriel

"Behold the handmaid of the Lord: be it unto me according to your word" (Luke 1:38 NKJV).

J esus, transcended from eternity to time, through the womb of a woman. It was in the year eight (8) B.C., (a number which for us means completeness, overflowing), when I received a startling visit from the angel Gabriel, in our humble home in the city of Nazareth in Galilee. The angel brought news that meant overflowing joy to the world. It was the fullness of time, for the long awaited promised to be fulfilled, for Israel's Daystar to appear.

About thirty-three years ago, in the city of Nazareth in Galilee, I spent many days celebrating my engagement and maundering about wedding plans with the love of my life, Joseph. I was so fortunate to be getting married to a humble, godly man, who was of the house and lineage of King David (Luke 2:4).

Ever since our engagement, I woke up each day with thoughts of our soon-to-be happy lives together. I knew that God would bless us with a happy home where His presence would dwell. Since my engagement with Joseph, I even found myself drawing closer and closer to God asking Him to help me to be a good wife and to bless our home with children. Many times, I would quietly sing the words penned by our Psalmist, "Blessed is everyone that fears the Lord...Thy wife shall be as a fruitful vine by the sides of thine house: thy children like olive plants round about thy table" (Psalm 128).

I knew that I needed the help of my heavenly Father to become a good wife. Soon after, I would stop singing about my own interests and start praising the one I love the most, Yahweh my Father in heaven.

One day, while I was at home, singing Psalms of praise and thanksgiving at home, and thinking about wedding preparations, I had a life changing encounter. I was startled as I noticed a heavenly body standing before me. I felt the hair on my head rising. My eyes squinted at the sudden burst of radiant light.

"Mary," I heard the voice calling gently from the light. "You are highly favoured by God, and the Lord is with you. Blessed are you among women."

"What do you mean?" I enquired, in a state of awe.

Though the light was bright and scintillating there was a lovely warm energy emanating from the unexpected visitor. That energy gave me courage to speak although I was bewildered. I peered into the light and spoke again. "Who are you?" I asked, trembling a little. Then a gentle response came, "Fear not Mary, I am the angel Gabriel. You are blessed and highly favoured."

But why would he say such a thing? "What is the purpose of this visit?" I could not help but wonder if he came to bring an answer to a prayer, however, I could not recall praying and asking God for anything specific, except for me to live a life that was pleasing to Him and to have a good and happy marriage with Joseph. Those were some of the main prayer requests most women who lived in Israel at that time would take to God's throne of grace. Still I was bemused and astonished that an angel would visit me.

Looking at my troubled face, the angel spoke again, tenderly yet expressively, as if making a declaration.

"I have come to tell you that above all women you are a chosen vessel. You have been chosen by our Heavenly Father to bring forth his Son. You shall conceive and bring forth a son, and shall call his name Jesus." Then he continued talking and sounded like he was even chanting.

"Your son Jesus shall be great, and shall be called the Son of the Highest. And the Lord shall give unto him the throne of his father David: He shall reign over the house of Jacob forever and of his kingdom there shall be no end" (Luke 1:32-33).

"How can this be? I am not yet married," I queried. "Besides, I am a virgin."

"Yes, I knew you would ask," replied the angel. "The Holy Spirit will come upon you. The power of the Highest shall overshadow you and shall place a seed in your womb. Therefore, the Holy child that shall be born of you shall be called the Son of God,"

"Mary," the angel continued, "it will happen to you just as I said. Your cousin Elizabeth has conceived in her old age. She who was barren is now six months pregnant. For with God nothing is impossible."

One thing was sure, I knew that I wanted God's will to be done in my life. I also wanted to be used by him. We cannot predict what will happen when we say 'yes' to God. I desired nothing else than God's perfect will to be done in my life, whatever the cost. My prayer has always been that I will please my Lord in all my ways. What an opportunity this was for me to please my Lord. My answer to the angel Gabriel was without hesitation, "Behold, the handmaid of the

Lord: be it unto me according to your word" (Luke 1:38).

No sooner I said these words the angel of the Lord departed.

Not long after, I felt the presence of the Lord overshadowing me and I knew that the Holy seed was occuring in my womb at that time, just as the angel foretold. I, the Virgin Mary, had become pregnant. What an incredible miracle!

3.

Visit to Cousin Elizabeth

"…as soon as the voice of your greeting sounded in my ears, the
babe leaped in my womb for joy"
(Luke 1:44 NKJV).

I was excited and yet afraid. thoughts of what everyone would say clouded my mind, for a moment, because I was pregnant and not married.

What about Joseph? How would he react to all this? I hoped that he would believe me when I told him that my baby was a gift from God, and that I was carrying the Son of God in my womb. Surely, Joseph would recall the writing of the prophets telling that our Saviour had to come to earth, through the seed of a woman, to save His people from their sins. Then I thought of the law which stated that I could be stoned to death for becoming pregnant and not for my fiancé Joseph.

These intimidating thoughts rested on my mind momentarily, however, I was soon comforted with thoughts of the greatness of Yahweh and His ability to take care of me, His servant. I knew the Christ child had to be born and it was settled in my spirit that it would be all right.

Still feeling a bit overwhelmed, I wanted to get away, to find a place where I could ponder more about what the angel had told me and to find a place of solace. It was then that I decided to visit my cousin Elizabeth whom the angel said was miraculously pregnant in her old age. I also wanted to talk to someone about what the angel told me, and who better than Elizabeth, as she was so devout to God, a mother of Israel who was full of godly wisdom. I knew she would believe my every word.

Therefore, I wasted no time in telling my parents and Joseph about my plans to visit cousin Elizabeth. I packed a few items and was soon off.

It was such a joy to be visiting my dear cousins at their home in the quiet country side of Judah. How surprising that no sooner I saluted Elizabeth she turned to me with a glowing face and shouted out joyfully, "Blessed art thou among women, and blessed is the fruit of thy womb. And why should I have such privilege that the mother of my Lord should visit me" (Luke 1:42).

From the thrill in her voice, I could tell that she was filled with the Holy Spirit and could not contain herself. She explained that as soon as she heard my voice calling her, the baby in her womb leaped for joy. What a divine encounter it was! I, too, soon became flooded with tears of joy. Then, one of Israel's songs of rejoicing sprang up in my heart, and I started to sing it with exuberance, no doubt as Hannah did when the song of praise was first given to her on the birth of Samuel, Israel's first and distinguished prophet.

My soul doth magnify the Lord,
And my spirit rejoices in God my Saviour.
For He has regarded the low estate of His handmaiden:
For behold, from henceforth all generations shall call me blessed,

For he that is mighty hath done to me
great things;

And Holy is his name.

And His mercy is on them that fear Him
from generation to generation

He hath shewed strength with his arm;

He hath scattered the proud in the imagi-
nation of their hearts.

He hath put down the mighty from their
seats, and exalted them of low degree

He hath scattered the proud in the imagi-
nation of their hearts.

He hath put down the mighty from their
seats,

And exalted them of low degree.

He hath filled the hungry with good
things;

And the rich he hath sent empty away.

He hath holpen his servant Israel,

In remembrance of his mercy;

As he spake to our fathers, to Abraham, and to his seed forever (Luke 1:46-55 NKJV).

Oh, how delighted I felt in the presence of my precious cousin, dear Elizabeth! We both sang songs of joy, praising the Lord for the way He was using us and what the birth of our sons would mean for Israel and the people of the world. My time spent with Elizabeth simply cheered my heart and strengthened me for the journey ahead.

Elizabeth told me the story about the glorious visit by the same angel Gabriel, as was explained to her by her husband. She showed me the script which her husband Zacharias wrote sharing the story of the angel's visit with the news that they will have a baby in their old age, as he was unable to speak since the visit of the angel. She explained to me that her husband, cousin Zacharias, was serving in the temple when suddenly, through the burning incense, he saw an angel.

According to Elizabeth, Zacharias was overcome with fear, but the angel said unto him:

"Fear not, for thy prayer is heard; and thy wife Elizabeth shall bear thee a son, and you shall call his name John" (Luke 1:13).

Elizabeth told how the angel said that their son, John, would go before the Messiah in the spirit and power of Elias, to turn many of the people of Israel's hearts to the Lord."

Cousin Elizabeth's child would be very special and grow to become Israel's greatest and last prophet. He would prepare the way for the Lord, my son. He was that forerunner that Isaiah wrote about 'the voice of him that crieth in the wilderness, prepare ye the way of the Lord, make straight in the desert a highway for our God' (Isaiah 40:3).

John surely grew up to do just that, preaching in the wilderness calling the people of Israel to repentance, turning their hearts to the Lord and baptising them.

Sadly, cousin Zacharias did not believe the words of the angel. For both he and Elizabeth had long passed the age of having children. They had been barren for so long that Zacharias the priest, did not think this was possible. But I can never forget the words of the angel who first told me that my cousin Elizabeth would soon have a baby in her old age. When I wondered how could this be, the angel Gabriel said sternly, 'with God nothing is impossible' (Luke 1:37).

I spent three blissful months with my cousin Elizabeth who taught me many things I needed to know about womanhood to help prepare me to be a good mother to my son and a wonderful wife to Joseph, one day. We spent much time praying together and praising God for our miracle babies. I left her home feeling lifted and ready for the next step of the journey especially since on my return home, everyone would soon notice my pregnancy.

Oh, they would be asking many questions, and of course throwing many accusations. One thing I was sure of, God will give me strength to go through whatever I may have to face for being pregnant and unmarried. He has already given me a song of praise to keep me joyful, which I will continue to sing all my days, 'My soul doth magnify the Lord. And my spirit rejoices in God my Saviour...' Singing unto the Lord made my heart glad. I was determined to hold on to my song of praise for I have proven Nehemiah 8:10 and can truly say that *the joy of the Lord is my strength.*

4.

Not Everyone Believed

"But as many as received Him, to them He gave the right to become children of God, to those who believe in His name" (John 1:12 NKJV).

As anticipated, the rumour started to circulate around the neighbourhood about my being pregnant for another man and that I had been unfaithful to my fiancé Joseph. I was the talk of the town. Women would roll their eyes at me, others stared at me wherever I would go to the market, the well and even the temple. Yet none of the whispering moved me because Yahweh had strengthened me for it all. I remained pleasant and graceful to all those who were judging me wrongfully, for it was my prayer to God, that I do not become bitter but be filled with his grace at all times.

I did not mind what others thought of me or their look of disdain at my rising stomach, for I knew 'who' I was carrying. Their frowning faces did not move me, for I knew too it came from a lack of understanding. It was when Joseph, my dear Joseph, whom I so loved and trusted, did not believe my story, that I felt most distraught. Although we were not yet officially married, he was, in the eyes of God and man, my husband and I his wife, by Jewish rites.

"Mary, I know you to be the most virtuous girl there is, but how can I believe that you are pregnant by God's Holy Spirit?" Joseph said those painful words to me, after I confided in him about the angel's visit. I told very few people, for I know that not many people understand the things of God and would believe. So, I often pondered the things the angel said to me and allowed the words to strengthen my faith in God.

"How can I make Joseph believe?" I recognised that I could not. The impossible had happened to me, a virgin had become pregnant! My prayer was that our heavenly Father would reveal His truth to Joseph.

By now he made it plain that he felt hurt and let down, and that he had to put me away secretly, for he loved me too much to have the elders of Israel throw stones at me. But still his heart could not take the betrayal. I remained silent and prayerful while he shared his most inner thoughts with me. I realised that there was nothing I could have done to persuade him. Feeling heartbroken that Joseph, the love of my life, was now breaking up with me, I could not hold back the tears. I started to cry in his arms, and he caressed me gently then walked away, whispering goodbye. However, I regained strength, looked up to heaven, asked the Lord to have mercy upon me his handmaid, and let His will be done in my life.

"Father," I prayed, "if Joseph is to be my husband, then you must speak to him yourself, about the angel's visitation. For how can I raise this child by myself? I am only but a young girl, I need the help of a just man like Joseph to be in your Son's life."

I was ready to storm the heavens for my Joseph, and then a sweet calm came over me. It was like an angel came to strengthen me, and I simply said, "Lord let your will be done in my life." Soon after, I laid down and fell asleep.

Truthfully, I fell asleep with tears rolling down my eyes, but firmly trusting in God. God's people can always fall asleep with a verse of hope hovering over their minds. That night I went to sleep with Psalm 30:5 on my mind, 'weeping may endure for the night, but joy comes in the morning. I took God at His word and was expecting joy in the morning."

"In the morning, before dawn there was a knock on my door. It was Joseph, he came to tell me that God had revealed to him in a dream that night, that I was telling the truth. I believe, while I was praying, Yahweh sent an angel to speak to him in his dream. Joseph shared with me the words of the angels "Joseph, son of David, fear not to take unto thee Mary thy wife: for that which is conceived in her is of the Holy Ghost" (Matthew 1:20).

Oh, how overjoyed I felt and we both wept in each other's arms and shed tears of joy, for God had worked miraculously to keep us united. Joseph apologised with tears in his eyes for not believing my words. He confessed that he should have known better, for the way I lived my life before him and Yahweh, not that I was perfect. Joseph also shared that that night he got up and searched the Torah and found where Isaiah wrote stating that a virgin shall bring forth a son who shall rule over all and his kingdom will have no end (Isaiah 7:14). He also said that Yahweh reminded him of the prophecy written by Moses in Genesis 3:15, "and I will put enmity between thee and the woman, and between thy seed and her seed; it shall bruise thy head, and thou shalt bruise his heel," he quoted. Then my loving Joseph placed his hand on my shoulder and said, "Mary you are the woman, carrying the seed that will crush the head of our enemy, once and for all."

Joseph spoke again, this time down on his knee, reaching out for my hand, he looked directly into my face and asked ever so sweetly, "Mary would you marry me? I shall be at your side all the way to help you raise the holy child."

"Of course, I shouted with exuberance! Yes, yes, my Joseph."

God knows when we need to be supported by a man or a woman. Today, I thank him for Joseph's commitment to stand by my side at this critical season in my life. Joseph is not only my fiancé and soon to be husband, he had become my Aaron and Hur, helping to hold me up.

Joseph promised that he would search all the scriptures concerning our son, so that he could better understand the will of God for us. I told him that my story is hard to believe. And that I knew that not everyone would believe but what is important is that God's people would believe and accept the Christ child as their Saviour. "I am only God's handmaiden," I said. "I cannot make men believe the things that God has revealed to me that is why I reflect frequently on the message of the angel and joyfully meditate on them in my heart."

Joseph realised that he, too, was chosen as the earthly father to care for God's Son. He fell on his knees right away, laid his hands on my tummy and started to pray. He asked God for wisdom, good health and strength, for a loving and peaceful home that we would be able to raise His son that he entrusted to us. We had a quiet wedding shortly after, but Joseph reverend the Christ Child that was in my womb and our marriage was not consummated until after the birth of Christ.

Oh, how we became rejuvenated and excited about making preparations for the baby. Joseph started preparing our little home in Nazareth for his birth. He was a skilful carpenter and made a beautiful crib for our precious baby. Then he started making many different animal shaped wooden toys, mostly sheep, horses, and cows. "These are all for him," he said, "I want him to be happy in our home. And I hope that one day, we will make beautiful wooden things together too".

"I'm sure you both will," I replied, "after all, He is the creator of the universe and you are the best carpenter I know. What a combination of talent that will be!" And we both chuckled with joy.

Oh, how sweet to trust our heavenly Father. Each time I face daunting situations, I was assured by scripture, 'weeping may endure for the night, but joy comes in the morning.' (Psalm 30:5). Joy was also on its way to a troubled, weeping world. Oh, and how much joy my Son brought to all mankind—yes, indeed, joy to the world!

5.

The Prophecy of the Birth Place

"But you, Bethlehem Ephrathah, though you are little among the thousands of Judah, Yet out of you shall come forth to Me The One to be Ruler in Israel, Whose goings forth are from of old, From everlasting" (Micah 5:2, NKJV).

"Still one thing was strange," said Joseph, "remember how I've told you that I will be searching out the Torah concerning prophecies about our Messiah? Well, Micah has made it quite clear that the Messiah should be born in Bethlehem, I even memorized his prophecy. Micah 5:2 says: "But you, Bethlehem Ephratah, though you are small among the clans of Judah, out of you will come for me one who will be ruler over Israel, whose origins are from of old, from ancient times."

While we prepared our home in Nazareth to raise the Christ Child, our minds were also set on travelling to Bethlehem, we just did not have the details on the whole matter. Truthfully, we still did not feel the urgency to leave. It will have to be God's doing.

Not long after, there went out a decree by Governor, Caesar Augustus, that everyone should be taxed in his own city. This meant that Joseph and I had to travel to Bethlehem, since he was of the house of the lineage of David and be registered to pay taxes in Bethlehem. I never questioned God why so near the time of my delivery, we had to travel so far from Galilee out of the city of Nazareth, into Judaea, into the city of David, Bethlehem, for I knew that the Holy Scriptures must be fulfilled. Joseph and I packed the necessities for the journey and departed on our donkey to Bethlehem, we knew that the purpose of our journey to Bethlehem was not just to register for taxation, but that the words of prophecy must be fulfilled, concerning the birth place of the Messiah, as was written by Micah.

6.

Christ is Born

"For there is born to you this day in the city of David a
Saviour, who is Christ the Lord"
(Luke 2:11, NKJV).

It was an arduous journey travelling to Bethlehem on our donkey near the time of my delivery. You could imagine how thrilled we were when we arrived in the town of Bethlehem. We longed for a little comfort and could not wait to get to the closest inn. From the motion I was feeling in the womb, I sensed that anytime now, baby Jesus was ready to enter the world.

Further, my dear Joseph also needed to rest. Much of his time on the journey, was spent caring for me and ensuring I was comfortable riding on the donkey. He exerted much energy on the gruelling ninety-mile journey, from Galilee, out of the city of Nazareth, into Judea, to the city of David, the town Bethlehem, it was telling on him. My Joseph was looking a little worn and I heard him panting softly and gasping for breath occasionally.

Yet, as exhausted as we were, we just had to give God thanks and praise for giving us the strength and for keeping us safe each step of the way. I was certain that a host of angels was with us throughout the entire journey. And I had a song of praise to keep me on the way, "My soul magnifies the Lord..." A song of praise always, causes joy to bubble in our hearts. Joy that is needed for the journey.

By God's grace we made it to Bethlehem. The joy of arriving in Bethlehem gave us a sudden surge of energy to move swiftly towards the inn, to book a room. We could not believe our ears when we learnt that there was no room in the inn. It was disappointing news. We were informed that all the other inns were filled as there were many visitors in Bethlehem on account of the census. Yet, hope remained alive in us as we were confident that Jehovah who brought us here, had a place for us to stay. The truth is, the time of delivery was here. Joseph persuaded the innkeeper to make space available somewhere on his property for us, as I was expecting to give birth anytime and was in no condition to travel any further.

shall be to all people, for unto you is born this day in the city of David a Saviour who is Christ the Lord,'" said another shepherd.

Yet, another shepherd could not wait to raise his staff to speak, "Then the angel told us that we would find the babe wrapped in swaddling clothes, lying in a manger. Wow, we can always depend on the words of God's Holy angels. Look, there is our Saviour wrapped in swaddling clothes and laying in a manger. We know He is indeed our Messiah."

"But that is not the end of the story, for then suddenly a host of angels appeared around us, and started praising and worshipping God in our presence. It was a sight to behold," said the smallest shepherd among them. "I also remembered the song they sang." Then they all raised their staffs and started singing, "Glory to God in the highest and on earth peace, goodwill toward men."

Of course, Joseph and I soon joined in with the shepherds and sang lustily.'

"Glory to God in the highest and on earth peace, goodwill toward men."

"We knew that something special and significant must have happened in the earth this night. We made haste to move quickly to find the Saviour for ourselves. Praise be to God, for coming to lowly shepherds and telling us about the birth of His Son. And now we will tell the news to everyone, everywhere we go, that Israel's Messiah, the Saviour of the world is born!" said the eldest shepherd. "Now we must be on our way to spread the good news," he concluded.

Humbly, we thanked the shepherds for coming and bid them farewell. Joseph blessed them pronouncing the sacred Hebrew blessing over their lives:

> The LORD bless you and keep you;
> The LORD make His face shine upon
>   you,
> And be gracious to you;

The LORD [a]lift up His countenance
   upon you,
And give you peace" (Numbers 6:24-
26, NKJV).

As I held our Messiah in my arms, and reflected on the visit of the humble shepherds, words from Isaiah sprang up forcefully in me, and I declared it out loudly in the stable.

The Spirit of the Lord is upon Him,
because He is anointed to preach good
   tidings to the poor,
He is here to heal the brokenhearted,
to proclaim the acceptable year of the
Lord, and the day of vengeance of our
   God, to comfort all who mourn,
to console those who mourn in Zion,
   to give beauty for ashes,
   the oil of joy for mourning,
   the garment of praise for the spirit of

heaviness
that they may be called trees of
righteousness,
the planting of the Lord, that He may be
glorified" (Isaiah 61: 1-3).

What can I say? A wonderful Saviour is here!

7.

Our Child is Named

"And she will bring forth a Son, and you shall call His name JESUS, for He will save His people from their sins" *(Matthew 1:21, KJV).*

We moved out of the barn and headed back to our home in Nazareth, not long after the visit of the shepherds. We had to prepare for His circumcision and later, to offer our boy child up in the temple, according to the law of Moses. We ensured that the Christ child observed all the Jewish traditions that pleased His heavenly Father. The first business according to our tradition, was for the Christ Child to be circumcised and named.

Heeding the tradition set for all Hebrew baby boys, on the eighth day, we circumcised our Son, and named Him 'Jesus' as the angel said he should be called.

Jesus is a most beautiful name. In Hebrew, we say Yeshua, which means, "God is Salvation," for He shall save His people from their sins. Apart from Jesus, our Son had many other names by which he could also be called. In Genesis, He is well known as the Seed of a Woman (Genesis 3:15).Moses also referred to him as, 'the Prophet whom everyone should listen to' (Deuteronomy 18:15).

Then Isaiah gave him many truthful names: Wonderful, Counsellor, Mighty God, the Everlasting Father, and the Prince of Peace. Isaiah also called him the Branch, the Arm of the Lord. Job called him Redeemer. The Psalmist called him Cornerstone while Solomon called him Rose of Sharon and the Lilly of the Valley.

Malachi referred to him as the 'Sun of Righteousness.' And of course, he was also named Emmanuel, which means God is with us, a name that brings much comfort and peace.

Christ was another special name for Him, which means the anointed one. All these names are very significant and special in meaning, speaking to the character of Christ. But the name that is most precious to me and I believe to His followers is the name Jesus. For in that name is the main purpose of His coming to earth, 'for He should save His people from their sins.'

How wonderful! Christ came to save and redeem us unto our heavenly Father, not only the people of Israel, but the world. Hear His beautiful words recorded by John, His beloved disciple "For God so loved the world that He gave His only begotten Son, that whosoever, believes in Him should not perish but have everlasting life (John 3:16)." Praise ye the Lord!

12.

Mary's Affirmation

"And He will reign over the house of Jacob forever, and of
His kingdom there will be no end" (Luke 1:33).

I know of his miraculous birth without any shadow of a doubt, He Who hung on the cross is the Messiah, the Saviour of the world. All who do not believe can ask my cousin Elizabeth, the shepherds, the wise men, Simeon and Anna and many others. It was God who chose to reveal to them the Good news concerning the birth of His Son. They were certain that He who hung on the cross is Jesus, the Christ, Israel's long-awaited Messiah, the Saviour of the world.

Today, I, Mary, the mother of God's Son, have no fear, I know that his crucifixion on the cross was not the end of Him, for I have always pondered, on the words of the angel Gabriel to this very day. He said one thing that I know to be true and that is, "Jesus' kingdom will have no end." Therefore, when I look up at my son bleeding from the cross, and I reflect on all the prophecies declared about my Lord, it conjured up a warm, peaceful feeling in my heart that had a mixture of tears of joy and sorrow flooding down my cheeks. Indeed, it may be the end of His sojourn with us on earth, but I know that it was not the end of Him who is God and is the resurrection and the life.

You shall call Him Jesus, because He will save His people from their sins. Though my heart is pained, yes pierced, looking up again at my Lord, I know that all is not lost. He is fulfilling His purpose. He is not just my Child; He is God's Son and the Saviour of the world. Joseph and I were humbled to serve as earthly parents to take care of God's most precious gift to the world.

Epilogue

"...Men of Galilee, why do you stand gazing up into heaven?
This *same* Jesus, who was taken up from you into heaven,
will so come in like manner as you saw Him go into heaven"
(Acts 1:11, NKJV).

I write this epilogue from the upper room where his faithful followers would often gather for prayer, while awaiting the outpour of the Holy Spirit. From this prayer room, there is much good news to share in closing. The truth because of Christ's finished, redemptive work at the cross of Calvary, and His glorious resurrection, both of which I witnessed, I am no longer mournful about His sacrificial atonement at the cross. Not only am I seated in the upper room, but through the cross, I am also now seated in 'heavenly places with Christ my Lord'.

Now, I reflect on Isaiah's prophecy about Christ sufferings, with gratitude and thankfulness that, "...he was wounded for our transgressions, he was bruised for our iniquities: the chastisement of our peace was upon him; and with his stripes we are healed" Isaiah 53:5. Another prophecy, that solidifies, that Jesus Christ, born of a woman, is the Son of the living God.

Friends, the good news is that Christ is no longer in a manger, nor is He still hanging on the cross. I am exuding with delight, for I hasten to record that we have seen our risen Lord! Not surprisingly, the women were the first to have had an encounter with our risen Lord.

Our mission now is to serve him and to carry out his commandment through the spreading of the gospel which tells of His saving grace. We are making preparations in prayer, waiting for Him to empower us to carry out that great commission:

Go ye therefore, and teach all nations, baptizing them in the name of the Father, and of the Son, and of the Holy Ghost:

Teaching them to observe all things whatsoever I have commanded you: and, lo, I am with you always, even unto the end of the world. Amen (Matthew 28:19, 20).

Like the shepherds who left their flock to come to the manger, so too, we have to give up our regular routine, and make haste with the message of salvation. The clarion call must ring out loudly, that Jesus is the answer for the world today. It is a call to 'leave the world' and follow our risen Lord and Saviour.

From His miraculous conception in my womb, to His glorious resurrection after being crucified on the cross, there is absolutely nothing about Jesus' life on earth that was ordinary. The Son of Mary, born in Bethlehem, was 'God in flesh', to use the words of His beloved disciple John.

The baby of Bethlehem grew up and demonstrated who He was to the world. He fulfilled the written oracles concerning His life on earth. Jesus died, was buried and was the first to be resurrected from the dead in a new body. After His time on earth was over, He returned to His Father in heaven.

He is now seated in power at His Father's right hand. There, He continues to show His love for us, as He ever intercedes for the redeemed, but that is not the end. I have something very important to add to the story about Jesus. One day, He will return for all the people of His Kingdom. One day, Christ will return to earth for all those who believed in Him and lived for Him. Hear the words of the angels to those who saw Him ascending into heaven:

> Ye, men of Galilee, why stand ye gazing up into heaven? This same Jesus, which is taken up from you into heaven, shall so come in like manner as ye have seen him go into heaven.(Acts 1:11).

In awe, we saw so many prophecies written in the Torah about our Lord fulfilled. Our experience has taught us to take seriously the words of prophecy spoken by the angels while Jesus was ascending to heaven. For certain, just as the angels declared, Jesus will return to earth one day, we can expect these words to come to pass. And what a day that will be! My friends, do not doubt who He is, like all those who shouted 'crucify

Him.' Instead, shout in like manner as His disciple Peter, when He was sinking in the ocean, "Jesus Save Me!" Let the words of the angel Gabriel, that were spoken to me many years ago, resonate with you, "You shall call His name Jesus, for He shall save His people from their sins." Friends whosoever shall call on the name of the Lord, shall be saved! Oh, how beautiful it is for me to know that my Son became my Saviour.

My friends, I recommend Him to you: to you the shepherds of the world, to you the wise men, to you the priests, to you the inn keepers, to you the Herods of this world, and weeping women. I wish for all to come to know Him, for He came to give us new life that we can only experience in Him, through the power of His blessed Holy Spirit. Indeed, all who come and follow Him shall live and reign with Him, one day in His Eternal Kingdom. There we will forever enjoy fellowshipping in His presence. Hallelujah!

Though the sword has pierced my heart, what a privilege it has been for me, a lowly woman of

Nazareth, to be the mother of God's Son, God's greatest gift to the world. Although I have shared my story, it was summed up best as written by John the beloved, "For God so loved the world that He gave His only begotten Son, that whosoever believeth in Him, should not perish, but have everlasting life. He did not come to condemn the world but that the world through Him might be saved" (John 3:16-17).

Verily, verily I say unto you, you can count on the words of a mother, this story is true, Jesus Christ of Nazareth, born in Bethlehem, the City of David, is the Saviour of the World. I bid you to accept Him as your Lord. Once you do, you too, will have many stories of His goodness to tell to the world.

Truly, truly, this is a true story, about my son Jesus.

Acknowledgements

All thanks and praise to Almighty God for placing this seed in my heart to explore the Nativity story from Mary's perspective. I am thankful for those who looked at the manuscript and encouraged me to publish.

Sincerest gratitude to Ricardo O. Henry, ordained Bishop, Church of God, Tampa, Florida for writing the Foreword for this book.

Special gratitude to my daughter Kadeise Hendrickson, an English teacher, who always finds time to review my work and assist with the first stage of editing. I am also grateful to Dr. Alson B.H. Percival, Archdeacon Emeritus, one of my former Bible teachers, for his comments and encouragement on reviewing the manuscript.

Thanks to my son, Kleeton Hendrickson and his family who are always very supportive of my book projects. Thanks to my own mother, Bernadine Webbe, with whom I spend quality time while working on the publication of this book, for her patience in allowing me time to sit around her house on my computer morning and evening and not expressing any annoyance.

To my sister, Shermel Webbe and her family, my immediate and extended family, thank you for being there to support me at the birthing stage of this book. My gratitude is also extended to my precious friend, Sister Jackie Jacobs, a writer herself, thank you for your invaluable feedback and words of encouragement.

A very special thank you, to Ms. C. Ruth Taylor, and her team at Extra Mile Innovators (EMI), who formalized the publication of "Mary Tells the Nativity Story of Prophecies Fulfilled" and making the path to publication a much easier and smoother process.

To everyone who would have encouraged or prayed for me along the way, thank you for your kind words and propelling, sustaining prayers.

May God reward all who have supported this work in anyway.

God's richest blessings. Shalom.

About the Author

Vanessa Webbe is passionate about sharing the good news of salvation whether through street evangelism, children's ministry or scribing inspirational thoughts. Ms. Webbe resides on the quiet, tranquil paradise island of Nevis, in the twin Island Federation of St. Kitts and Nevis. She is the mother of two children, Kadeise and Kleeton Hendrickson, and has three adorable grandchildren.

Her favourite hobbies include baking and gardening. Her heart's desire is to see people coming to the knowledge of who Christ is, experience the saving grace of the Lord Jesus Christ and the blissfulness of living in His presence.